What Our Readers Have Said...

Applicability

"These books are great tools that should be used as guidelines for our everyday supervisory practices. You need to take the time to do a short self-evaluation when reading them."

•

"The Pinpoint Training Series delivers information that could be used in a lot different areas."

•

"The things and problems we deal with everyday are discussed in these books."

Convenience

"I like this because I can take them with me to read at a convenient time. I feel the little time I have to spend in the office is best use on activities that directly relate to revenue opportunities. I like the short amount of time it takes to keep up with these."

•

"I prefer the self-study approach; it fits in with my schedule."

•

"I like the fact that the format allows the books to be reviewed as time permits. All work has been conducted on personal, evening/weekend time."

•

"Easy to use... if you put the time into it."

Challenge

"My thought is that the real value of these books comes into effect when doing the action plans."

•

"I like the fact that the format allows assignments to be reviewed as time permits."

Clarity

"Short and sweet. These books are easy to comprehend."

•

"Easy to use, understand, and reference if needed."

Relevance

"I have enjoyed reading these books. They are relevant to today's work environment and the ongoing change in the way we manage our workforce."

•

"I believe the contents of the Pinpoint series are excellent. It causes one to reflect on the daily dynamics in working with oneself as well as with management and peers."

Developing
Critical Thinking Skills

Pinpoint Leadership Skill Development Training Series

TIMOTHY F. BEDNARZ

BUSINESS PRESS

Pinpoint Leadership Skill Development Training Series
"Developing Critical Thinking Skills"
Timothy F. Bednarz

Graphic design: Monika Pawlak

Majorium Business Press
2025 Main Street
Stevens Point, WI 54481
715.342.1018 • 800.654.4935

ISBN 978-1-882181-03-2

Printed in the United States of America

Introduction

The Pinpoint Leadership Skill Development Training Series is designed for targeted training and education regarding increased improvement in a specific skill or competency.

Each book within this series is designed to be easy to use, understand and apply to your job. It can be used as a basis for training individuals, as a discussion guide or as a personal training tool.

Each chapter within this book discusses a specific concept. When you have completed all eight chapters you should have a 360º perspective of the topic.

Additionally, each chapter is divided into specific sections:

- The first section provides you with an overview of the topic
- The Implications section discusses why the concept is important, and why it is important to learn and apply.
- The Strategies, Tips & Techniques to Apply section teaches how to use and apply the particular concept to your work.
- The Points to Ponder section gives you something to think about or to be discussed with a group setting. These are questions not meant to be immediately answered, but to be pondered over time.
- The Training Activity section provides you with the tools to transfer what you have learned to your job. It is designed to help create an action plan to effectively apply the concept.

Each of the topics in this series is time-tested and proven in the marketplace. They have been used by thousands of employees as training tools. Many of the users have commented that what made these books valuable, was the ability to refer to them when a problem surfaced. They indicated that they remembered reading about the exact problem. They referred back to these books and found an appropriate solution.

You will find them equally valuable as a resource in your professional development library.

Table of Contents

LEARNING OBJECTIVES:

- The basis of critical thinking.

- How to develop, analyze and evaluate data and information through the use of critical thinking skills.

- How to effectively apply critical thinking skills to problem solving.

- How to effectively apply critical thinking skills to decision making.

- How to critically frame problems for accurate analysis.

- The appropriate application of specific critical thinking traits.

The Basics of Critical Thinking

Critical thinking can be defined as "learning to think better by improving one's thinking skills." Individuals who are critical thinkers use the thinking process to analyze (consider and reflect) and synthesize (piece together) what they have learned or are currently learning. Unfortunately, much of everyone's thinking tends to be biased, imprecise, unclear, uninformed or prejudiced. Since this becomes severely limiting, critical thinking is needed to improve its quality and value.

Within the organizational setting critical thinking is necessary for: overcoming problems, making changes, modifications or adaptations within work structures, methods and problem solving situations, resolving situational conflict and pressing issues, and inventing and implementing new ideas, techniques and solutions.

IMPLICATIONS — WHAT THIS MEANS TO YOU

Critical thinking development is a gradual process. It requires: mastering plateaus of learning as well as maintaining a serious focus on the process itself, changing personal habits of thought, which tends to be a long-range project, and extensive development time.

Within the process of critical thinking it is important to recognize what does not comprise its basic elements or components. Critical thinking is not accomplished by: saying something without carefully thinking it through, taking a guess at what one thinks "should" be done, memorizing material to analyze, discuss or examine, doing something just because it has always been done, believing something because it is what everyone else tends to believe, or arguing about something when there are no facts to back up the argument.

Critical Thinking Qualities

There are certain qualities critical thinkers possess and these characteristics tend to categorize individuals as "deep thinkers," which separates them from more typical "basic thinkers." Critical thinkers tend to be self-disciplined, self-directed, self-monitored and self-corrective thinkers. They raise essential or crucial questions and problems and then proceed to formulate them clearly and precisely. Critical thinkers gather, assemble, evaluate and appraise relevant information. They come to well-reasoned deductions, conclusions and solutions, while measuring and testing them against relevant standards and criteria. They also keep an open mind within alternative systems of thought while continually recognizing and assessing their assumptions and lines of reasoning. Finally, critical thinkers communicate effectively with others in seeking out and determining solutions for challenges and problems.

▨ STRATEGIES, TIPS & TECHNIQUES TO APPLY

There tends to be six developmental thinking phases that lead to "mastering" the art of critical thinking. Through extensive practice and applications of the process, individuals can expect to begin altering and eventually changing their individual habits of thought. Each progressive phase is described below.

Phase One: The **Unenlightened** Thinker — individuals generally are not consciously aware that significant problems do exist within their current patterns of thinking.

Phase Two: The **Confronted** Thinker — individuals are aware that existing problems are evident or apparent within their process of thinking.

Phase Three: The **Novice** Thinker — individuals try to initiate improvements within their thinking, but without relying on regular or consistent practice.

Phase Four: The **Proactive** Thinker — individuals do recognize the importance of regular practice to improve and enhance their thinking.

Phase Five: The **Developed** Thinker — individuals begin to advance in accordance with the amount of practice that is awarded to the process.

Phase Six: The **Mastery** Thinker — individuals become skilled and insightful, where reflective, analytical and evaluative thinking becomes second nature.

Individuals can only develop through these phases if they accept the fact that there are serious problems with their current processes and methods of thinking, and are able to accept the challenge that their thinking presents to them and make it a point to begin regular practice to improve and enhance the components and elements of critical thinking.

Critical Thinking Relies Upon Clarity of Purpose

In order to develop critical thinking, it is important for individuals to be clear as to the purpose of the task or topic at hand, and the main question that is at issue in regard to it. To accomplish this goal, it is essential to: strive to be clear, accurate, precise and relevant, practice thinking beneath the surface, be logical and fair-minded, apply critical thinking skills to all reading, writing, speaking and listening activities, and apply these skills to all aspects of work as well as life in general.

Questioning: The Impetus for Critical Thinking

Dead questions reflect dead minds. Unfortunately, most individuals, (even managers, leaders and trainers) tend not to ask many thought-stimulating types of questions. They tend to stick to dead questions like, "Is this going to be what is expected from now on?" or, "How are we supposed to understand (or do) this?" and other questions that outwardly imply the desire not to think.

Some managers, leaders, trainers or facilitators in turn are not themselves generators of in-depth questions and answers of their own making, which aids in establishing non-critical thinking environments. These individuals are not seriously engaged in thinking through or rethinking through their own initiatives, issues, concerns, topics or instructional concepts and resort to being mere purveyors of the "questions and answers of others." They often end up initiating or responding to some initial concerns or issues that tend to surface spontaneously during a discussion or meeting, without having personal background information that would otherwise help stimulate deeper levels of creative probing and evaluative questioning. Sometimes they tend to apply second-hand information, knowledge or questions that have been passed down, which limits creative assessments and deeper level questioning. Often they find themselves referencing authors or others who are considered to be experts or leaders in their field rather than questioning important workplace-related issues, ideas, methods or concerns that need to be probed in-depth.

Questioning Through Critical Thinking Keeps the Organization Alive

Every company stays alive only to the extent that fresh questions are generated and taken seriously. These questions are then used as the driving force for generating and implementing changes. To think through or rethink anything, individuals within an organization must ask questions that stimulate deeper levels of thought. Questions define tasks, express problems and identify issues. While answers on the other hand, often signal a full stop in thought. Only when answers generate further questions does thought continue to add value in terms of personal as well as organizational growth and change.

It is important to remember that individuals within an organization, who generate and ask serious and insightful questions, are the ones who are, in fact, truly thinking, developing and learning. It is possible to move an organization forward by just asking employees to list all of the questions that they have about an issue, method or topic, including all questions generated by their first list of questions. However, deep questions drive out thoughts that rest underneath the surface of things and force individuals to deal with complexity. While questions of purpose force individuals to define "their task," questions of information force individuals to look at their source(s) of information as well as its quality.

TRAINING ACTIVITY — APPLICATION & ACTION PLAN

There are two main questions that you should personally address and respond to when considering the critical thinking process.

- "How can I effectively develop as an avid critical thinker?"
- "How can we as a collective group of organizational members help ourselves to practice better thinking in everyday work situations as well as in our everyday life?"

Answer these two questions in order to discuss them with your manager, supervisor or peers, or in an active discussion group.

2

Why Organizations
Need Critical Thinkers

Within organizations a lack of critical thinking can be severely damaging. Critical thinking is needed for problem solving, and for generating innovative ideas and solutions. Without creative thinking new paths and avenues of direction fail to be fully explored and forged. When organizations lack creative thinkers, they tend to see that their working environments are made up of employees who: blindly repeat the destructive or negative reactions they have learned over previous histories of time and events, automatically accept at face value all justifications given by organizational superiors or peers, don't question existing workplace norms and boundaries, whether they are written or unspoken, beneficial or detrimental, robotically trust internal organizational goals, plans and initiatives, routinely accept and say that if "higher ups" within the organization say it, it must be so, and mechanically accept, believe and say that if the organization does it or promotes it, it must be right or appropriate.

Unfortunately many organizations do create or allow critical thinking limitations within themselves. At times this is unconsciously done by not openly challenging, debating or discussing important issues or topics with all involved employees. At others, ignoring the importance of critical thinking may be intentional in order to maintain or sustain rigid organizational control and compliance. Both are evidence of organizational shortsightedness, which creates severe limitations for the companies themselves, as well as for all who work within them.

It is far more effective to allow and encourage employees to use and apply their own work related knowledge and experience to help create changes that work to benefit everyone.

▓ IMPLICATIONS — WHAT THIS MEANS TO YOU

Within organizational environments that encourage and promote critical thinkers from within, workplaces are full of employees who apply:

Contextual sensitivity — Employees are sensitive to stereotypes and try to unconditionally accept others at face value.

Perspective thinking — Employees attempt to get into the "heads and minds" of others, where they are able to walk in the other person's shoes so as to see the world the way the other person views and perceives things.

Tolerance for ambiguity — Employees demonstrate the ability to accept multiple interpretations of the same situation.

Alertness to premature ultimatums — Employees are able and willing to invoke a powerful idea or concept, which inspires further debate and assessment.

▓ STRATEGIES, TIPS & TECHNIQUES TO APPLY

Master the Characteristics of Being an Effective Critical Thinker

There is another major reason why it is important to have critical thinkers within organizations. These individuals become the "movers and shakers" that act as the driving force for advancing things forward to obtain positive results.

As a critical thinker, it is important to seek out the truth and possess a spirited desire for the best knowledge, even if this knowledge upon obtaining it fails to support or ends up undermining their preconceptions, beliefs or self-interests. Critical thinkers are open-minded and possess a tolerance for divergent views, while at the same time actively monitor themselves for possible existing biases, partiality or preconceptions. They are analytical, insisting on reason and evidence, and are constantly alert to problematic situations since they are inclined to anticipate consequences. Critical thinkers are systematic and value organization, while adhering to purposeful focus and diligence in order to approach problems at all various levels of complexity. They have high self-confidence and trust their own reasoning skills and see themselves as being a good thinker. Critical thinkers are inquisitive and constantly curious and eager to acquire knowledge and learn explanations, even when the applications of the knowledge they glean is not immediately apparent. They possess cognitive maturity and excel at maintaining a sense of wisdom in making, suspending, or revising judgment. This is because of their awareness that multiple solutions can be acceptable. In addition they possess an appreciation of the need to reach closure even in the absence of complete knowledge.

Critical Thinkers Need to Incorporate Good Inductive and Deductive Reasoning

Critical thinkers are able to help their organization move ahead for one very important reason: They are good at "inductive and deductive" reasoning. Those who fail to invest time and effort in developing themselves to become more effective at inductive and deductive reasoning will have a much more difficult time analyzing, evaluating and extracting facts and information in a more sophisticated manner. This is what is necessary to reach appropriate and accurate assumptions, conclusions and solutions.

Critical thinkers need to use deductive reasoning to: reach a level of likely certainty about issues, arguments and topics, define or identify one critical argument from a variety of diverse facts, draw a conclusion that follows known facts that are stated within the premise of an issue, argument, topic or subject, rely on certainty that is based on a connection between and argument's premises and the conclusion drawn from them, determine a "valid argument" as compared to a "sound argument," and ascertain if the premises (reasons, facts, evidence, etc.) prove with absolute certainty that the conclusion is true, assuming the premises are true.

Critical thinkers use inductive reasoning to: derive a probable conclusion from the observation of diverse facts, learn from experience, generate an argument by using analogies, create hypothetical arguments, conclusions or solutions, and also ascertain a sense of certainty or uncertainty as to a conclusion, which is based on the given evidence, where they cannot establish any likelihood of realistic probability.

Critical Thinkers Must Become Masters of Language

Organizations depend upon active and open communication to achieve results as well as to maintain a sense of momentum, direction and synergy. Thinking without being able to transfer thoughts and reasoning into language and speech makes the whole process of critical thinking ineffective. This is why critical thinkers are so valuable. They take the communication process seriously and learn to use it effectively.

For critical thinkers, language needs to have three major functions, which must be applied effectively to: describe, inform and persuade. Persuasion is the manner by which individuals attempt to convince others to "their way of thinking" about a topic, idea, concept or method, where all logic, misleading or erroneous reasoning, and problem solving become involved. Critical thinkers must go about obtaining or promoting the facts in persuasive arguments to "get closer to the truth" and to set "the record straight." For critical thinkers, their language and words must be able to project factual but logical implications, and practical yet accurate impacts, while they swiftly discern abnormalities, manipulation or erroneous persuasions in the arguments of others.

Critical Thinkers Must Pay Careful Attention to "Language Forms"

As one of their abilities, critical thinkers need to be quick to pick up on emotionally charged language, as well as emotional meanings and implications, even though they themselves must tend to refrain from applying them unless they have a sound factual argument. They must also refrain from using, but be quick and alert to pick up on, manipulative language like cons, double talk and jargon. They also need to refrain from applying, but be quick to pick up on rhetorical devices, which include: slanting viewpoints or opinions, applying sly or misleading words, inserting implied or assumed verbal disclaimers, generating complicated or unclear and thoughts, and words and phrases that generate a highly emotional appeal for acceptance.

POINTS TO PONDER — SOMETHING TO THINK ABOUT

1. Do you feel your organization encourages and promotes critical thinking in its employees? Why or why not?
2. Who do you believe are the "movers and shakers" in your department or workplace for advancing things forward to obtain positive results? Do you believe they are considered critical thinkers? Why or why not?

TRAINING ACTIVITY — APPLICATION & ACTION PLAN

As a beginning point, identify one goal from those detailed below that you would like to meet in terms of improving your critical thinking skills.

Define why you feel it is more essential to focus on.

Keep this goal in mind as you think through problems, issues or topics.

- Be a self-disciplined, self-directed, self-monitored and self-corrective thinker
- Raise essential or crucial questions and problems and then proceed to formulate them clearly and precisely
- Gather, assemble, evaluate and appraise relevant information
- Come to well reasoned deductions, conclusions and solutions, while measuring and testing them against relevant standards and criteria
- Think open-mindedly within alternative systems of thought while continually recognizing and assessing their assumptions and lines of reasoning
- Communicate effectively with others in seeking out and determining solutions for challenges and problems

3

Requirements for Critical Thinking

ritical thinking can best be described as the capability of implementing an effective thinking process, which is typically considered as being "one specific type of reasoning process." While creative thinking is generally considered to be involved with the creation or generation of ideas, processes, experiences or objects, critical thinking is concerned with their evaluation. Critical and creative thinking are interrelated and complementary aspects of thinking and almost all of the thinking that is undertaken by individuals tends to contain some critical and some creative aspects and elements. For example, when an individual attempts to solve real life problems they tend to move back and forth several times between creative and critical reflection. As solutions begin to be developed, the associated consequences of them also begin to be analyzed and weighed. It is important when individuals attempt to improve their thinking abilities that they pay close attention to both the critical and creative aspects of the thinking process.

▓ IMPLICATIONS — WHAT THIS MEANS TO YOU

Critical as well as creative thinking and their associated processes are in reality, combinations of one's abilities, knowledge, values, attitudes, skills and processes. There are six cognitive skills that need to be used within critical and creative thinking: interpretation, analysis, evaluation, inference, explanation, and self-regulation.

While the base of knowledge that is required for critical and creative thinking tends to vary from topic to subject area, the underlying values and attitudes tend to remain constant across the spectrum of thinking and reasoning. There are distinguishing factors between "weak sense" and "strong sense" critical thinking and individuals who have the abilities necessary for undertaking quality critical and creative thought, but only tend to use them for their own advantage, are considered to be critical and creative thinkers in the weak sense. Where as individuals who tend to be classified as strong critical and creative thinkers are typically committed to using their abilities to seek out the most accurate and fair positions regardless of their own particular interests or desires. Their thinking takes into account the needs, viewpoints and arguments of others, which is built upon analysis of an individual's own motives.

STRATEGIES, TIPS & TECHNIQUES TO APPLY

Critical thinking in its truest sense relies upon "dialectical" reasoning, which involves thinking about the reasoning, motives and arguments of others and seeing all sides of a question and analyzing the strengths and weaknesses of opposing points of view. This type of thinking is accomplished by incorporating and utilizing the following foundational requirements, which are:

Interpretation

The criteria for good critical or creative thought in the area of knowledge and understanding tends to depend upon the methods developed for establishing the validity and truth of various claims. To interpret in an accurate and critical manner implies to comprehend and express meaning or significance as it relates to a wide variety of experiences, situations, data, events, judgments, conventions, beliefs, rules, procedures, or criteria. Critical thinking analyzes supportive claims, documentation or statements, where the brain sifts through information to make certain that it is not inaccurate, biased, misrepresented or false.

Analysis

To analyze through critical thinking implies identifying the intended and actual inferential relationships among statements, questions, concepts, descriptions, or other forms of representation meant to express belief, judgment, experiences, reasons, information, or opinion. There are certain types of questions that one needs to ask to effectively analyze and verify information and supportive documentation. Individuals should increasingly take responsibility for asking the types of questions below, not only to others, but also to themselves, in order to enhance their levels of knowledge and understanding so they are able to analyze and evaluate informational input much more thoroughly.

Questions that help to clarify:
Could you give me an example of _____? or, Is your basic point _____ or _____?

Questions that help to probe assumptions:
You seem to be assuming _____ is that correct? or, How would you justify taking this for granted? or, Is this always the case?

Questions that help to probe reasons and evidence:
How can we go about finding out whether that is true? or, Is there any reason to doubt this evidence?

Questions that help to discern viewpoints or perspectives:
How would other groups or types of people respond to this information? Why? What would influence them? or, How would people who disagree with this viewpoint or opinion argue their case?

Questions that probe implications and consequences:
What effect would (this or that) have? or, If this and this are the case, then what else must also be true?

Questioning a question:
To answer this question fully, what other questions would need to be addressed and answered first? or, Is this the same issue as _____?

Evaluation

Critical thinking uses evaluation to assess the credibility of statements or other representations. These are accounts or descriptions of a person's perception, experience, situation, judgment, belief, or opinion. Within critical thinking the aim is to accurately assess the logical strength of the actual or intended inferential relationships among various statements, descriptions, questions, or other forms of representation or documentation.

Inference

Within critical thinking, drawing an inference implies identifying and securing elements that are needed to make a reasonable conclusion about something. Inference is applied to: form conjectures and hypotheses, consider relevant information, and extract the consequences that tend to flow from data, statements, principles, evidence, judgments, beliefs, opinions, concepts, descriptions, questions, or other forms of representation.

Explanation

From a critical thinking perspective, an explanation implies stating the results of one's reasoning. The aim is to justify another's reasoning in terms of evidence, concepts, criteria, methodology, and context in which his or her results were based. Critical thinking relies upon presenting one's reasoning in the form of rational, strong, convincing and factual arguments while others begin to clarify it through reasoning, analysis and evaluation.

Self-Regulation

In relationship to critical thinking the term self-regulation implies the continuous monitoring of one's cognitive activities, the elements used in those activities, and the results produced. Self-regulation utilizes skills in the analysis and evaluation of one's own inferential judgments. The idea behind self-regulation is to reduce tendencies of generating biased interpretations and conclusions In regard to questions, confirming or validating information, or correcting another's reasoning or results.

Applying Critical Thinking Action Steps

Critical and creative thinking contribute to achieving crucial departmental, organizational as well as personal goals and objectives. In summarizing one's role in developing critical and creative thought processes, it is important to: understand the purposes underlying critical as well as creative thinking, believe in its potential benefits, and become increasingly reflective about one's own practice and habit of thinking in order to build the values, skills, knowledge and processes of critical and creative thinking into what he or she hears, observes and presents.

Think, act and respond in accordance with an ethical framework that reflects the qualities of honesty, integrity and compassion.

POINTS TO PONDER — SOMETHING TO THINK ABOUT

1. Why do you think critical thinking can be classified as one specific type of reasoning process?
2. What do you personally feel is a major difference between critical and creative thinking other than the definition that was offered within this lesson? Why?

TRAINING ACTIVITY — APPLICATION & ACTION PLAN

Critical thought is necessary for analyzing arguments and for rational decision making, while creative thinking is necessary in order to develop alternatives to concepts, ideas, or beliefs that are not considered to be desirable upon careful reflection.

Help to enhance and better develop your critical thinking abilities in order to move your personal self-development forward. In order to do this, follow some of these recommendations the next time you are involved in a discussion or situation that requires you to analyze, evaluate or judge information:

- Use the critical thinking process to attempt to solve a real work-related situation or problem where there is the possibility of more than one adequate solution, and where several different types of information are required.
- Use the vocabulary of critical thinking whenever discussing, questioning and presenting something.
- Use word or phrase qualifiers to help detail contradictions.
- Organize yourself for "structured controversy." Get involved in discussions and debates, which tend to tackle more than one side of an issue, remembering to back up arguments with evidence as well as reference to consequences.
- Ask some questions that require multiple answers, or several equally correct answers to help gain or establish deeper insights.
- Make it a point to defend your assertions with reasons.
- Follow another's answers, whenever appropriate, with a further question which asks why the individual believes the version he or she presented, or why the person thinks his or her answers are reasonable, plausible or accurate.
- Continually analyze the content of information for the accuracy and completeness of its portrayals, as well as the consistency of the reality and truth it presents.
- Continually use analogies and metaphors in descriptions, comparisons and attempts to understand new concepts, ideas, principles or theories.

4

Critical Thinking and Problem Solving

Critical thinking is essential to problem solving. The process of critical thinking allows individuals to draw assumptions, conclusions and solutions for existing problems and issues. However, to reach the point of effective critical thinking, a model should be developed and used to move the thinking process, as well as the evaluation of information, forward.

IMPLICATIONS — WHAT THIS MEANS TO YOU

It is impossible to reason and think critically and to solve pressing problems without using some set of facts, data, or experiences as an integral part of the thought and decision making process. Finding trustworthy sources of information and refining individual personal experiences are considered important goals when it comes to thinking critically. It is important to be vigilant about the sources of information that are used as the basis for one's reasoning and the subsequent arguments that work to support it within problem solving encounters. It is just as important to be "rationally and analytically critical" of one's own personal experiences.

Experience may be the best teacher, but biased experience only works to support bias, distorted experience only ends up supporting distortion, and self-deluded experience only effectively supports self-delusion. Since this is true, it is important not to think of personal experiences as being "sacred" but, instead, as one significant dimension of thought that must be like all others, critically analyzed, evaluated, weighed and assessed.

STRATEGIES, TIPS & TECHNIQUES TO APPLY

When it comes to solving problems, the mind must take in information in three distinctive ways:

- Internalizing inactive, lifeless or inert information into the mind that, though memorized, is not truly understandable or completely understood, despite the fact that individuals think they do comprehend it.
- Forming activated ignorance by taking into the mind and using information that is in reality false, even though individuals mistakenly think it to be true.
- Achieving activated knowledge and using this information that is not only true, but also when insightfully understood, generates expanded in-depth knowledge through its various implications.

An effective critical thinking problem solving model helps to generate needed information in the above three ways and aids in building a step-by-step approach to generate timely, workable and valuable solutions, outcomes or results.

The critical thinking process for problem solving needs to include addressing, researching and evaluating specific information that comes from identifying, defining and addressing problem solving content issues, which include:

- The description of the problem
- The factors or components of the problem (constructive vs. limiting)
- The ownership of the problem
- The scope of the problem
- The consequence of the problem
- Possible solutions for the problem
- One solution to implement

To work through the process the following procedures are important to incorporate.

Identifying, Defining and Addressing Process Issues Within the Problem Solving Activity

Several questions need to be asked: what is the level of self-awareness of the problem solver(s), how motivated is the problem solver(s), what form of decision making was involved in selecting solution(s) by solver(s), and finally, was the solution decided upon properly executed?

Identifying, Defining and Addressing Problem Solving Components of the Problem

All-encompassing components of the problem
- The size of the problem (costs, risks, losses etc.)
- Sensory input
- How does the problem look from an internal and external standpoint?
- How does the problem sound when it is accurately defined or described?
- How does the problem make people (employees, customers, etc.) feel?
- How does the problem affect organizational structures, methods, operations, etc.?

Identifying, Defining and Addressing Personal Components of the Problem

- Inside perspective of problem solver(s)
- Level(s) of personal concern over the problem
- The level(s) of self-esteem and confidence in regard to the problem solving process
    - o Low self-esteem of problem solver(s) is the hidden detrimental component of problem solving, which must be addressed to ensure productive solutions and outcomes

Identifying and Addressing Procedures
That Make the Problem Solving Process Work Effectively

- Unconditional acceptance & non-judgmental attitudes of all inclusive problem solvers
- Respect for each participant's input
- Freedom to openly express emotional responses to the problem as well as its solution(s)
- Defined limits and boundaries in regard to the problem solving process

Identifying, Defining and Addressing
Creativity in Problem Solving

Keep in mind that in order to create the desire to be a creative, and critical thinker, you as an individual must want to participate in the process. It is essential to maintain a focus on the importance of expanding knowledge and skills of language in order to be a more creative thinker. Remember that it takes effort to be creative in ones thinking and a critical evaluator of information, and that genius is comprised of being "1% inspiration and 99% perspiration" (Thomas Edison). It is necessary to ferment creativity — the process needs to be given time to generate results. Evaluate and validate all creative ideas and suggestions through brainstorming or "starbursting" to generate new viewpoints of information.

Keep in mind the "rules" for problem solving brainstorming: set a time frame to be completed, be clear what problem is to be solved, all ideas should be heard, accepted and considered, no idea is too outrageous to be expressed, quantity is desired; each idea coming to mind should be expressed, combining ideas for improvement is highly desirable, and criticism or a negative discussion regarding ideas must be absolutely forbidden.

There are also "rules" for problem solving starbursting: focus on a topic and expand it outward through continuous questioning, within the process, stress that "anything goes," make certain that all reasonable questions are considered legitimate, adhere to the philosophy, "the more questions the better," and begin by asking, "What are the questions?"

Complete a Critical Path Analysis

Once enough problem solving information is gathered it becomes necessary to determine the scope and length of the problem solving activity. It is important to be careful about time constraints and the available time to work on the problem solving task. It is wise to include expanding initial timetable expectations, since most tasks take far longer than initially anticipated.

Begin this process by:
- Calculating the length of time to complete the project;
- Listing all activities in the plan by: start date, duration, and whether or not activities are parallel or sequential;
- Define if certain tasks are dependent, and if so, what they depend upon;
- Graph the problem solving project out;
- Plot tasks on graph;
- Schedule activities;
- Define the project's critical path, in other words the longest sequence of dependent activities that lead to the completion of the plan.

Reinforce Applying Engagement Within the Problem Solving Method

Tap into problem solvers who have had a history of success with similar problems as well as those who have had a history of failure with similar problems and use this information to look at why failures occurred, and identify what things influenced the causes of failure. Rather than dismiss possible cause and effect relationships as well as internal and external influences that need to be factored into the existing problem, engage the problem by getting absorbed into it. Be willing to take the time to deal with the problem.

There are rules of engagement when dealing with problems. As such, it is important to become sensitive to your own confusion about a problem. Do not permit yourself to be or become confused, and do not tolerate confusion. Use visual imagery to help remember facts and information. Relate the information to specific people, events or situations. Make your visualization vivid, dynamic, interactive, & unusual.

Engagement in problem solving takes effort to deal with it, time to mull it over and looking squarely at the problem and not looking away from it.

Use the brainstorming process to identify, define and determine or verify:
- Possible solutions
- Alternative solutions
- A ranking or order of solutions
  - Through consensus arrive at the best, most workable solution

POINTS TO PONDER — SOMETHING TO THINK ABOUT

1. How do you currently go about solving a problem? Do you have a specific structure you follow? If so, what is it?
2. How does critical thinking help to improve the brainstorming process for solving problems? Can you think of one example?

TRAINING ACTIVITY — APPLICATION & ACTION PLAN

Decide on one problem that needs to be solved.

After identifying it, use critical thinking skills and techniques to walk yourself through the basic problem solving process that follows the steps of:
- Describing the problem thoroughly and accurately
- The factors or components of the problem (constructive vs. limiting)
- The ownership of the problem
- The scope of the problem
- The consequence of the problem
- Possible solutions for the problem
- One solution to implement

5

Critical Thinking
and Decision Making

It is essential to have a fundamental understanding of how critical thinking works within the decision making process. Critical thinking is a major part of any decision making process which helps to identify specific and accurate information to apply during the decision making life cycle and create a framework for managing a decision making issue, from its identification to its resolution.

Critical thinking tends to follow a five step scientific process and approach within the decision making and problem solving process, which includes identifying and developing: an accurate definition of a problem, a method for testing the problem's hypotheses, a focus on the facts, ways to analyze the problem by using various applicable questioning and verifying techniques, and an effective solution recommendation.

IMPLICATIONS — WHAT THIS MEANS TO YOU

Defining a Problem Needs to Be Done
Within a Critical Thinking Framework

A problem is a situation that is judged as being something that needs to be corrected. It implies that a state of "wholeness" does not exist within a situation or circumstance at the current time. It is the job of decision makers to make sure they are solving or acting upon the right problem or issue, and not necessarily the one presented to them as initially prescribed. From a critical thinking point of view, two questions become obvious: "What is it that truly needs to be decided upon?" and then, "What action needs to be taken?"

Most problems or issues can be initially identified by concerned individuals who are directly affected by the lack of something needed to improve their circumstances or abilities to produce more or generate more than they are currently capable of doing. Clearly defining a problem undoubtedly improves the focus of decision makers and also tends to drives the critical thinking process, which leads to a careful analysis of it.

Getting to a clearly defined problem is often discovery driven and it begins with a conceptual definition and through a critical analysis process, which includes root cause, impact analysis, etc. The problem then becomes reshaped and redefined in terms of intertwined and related issues.

STRATEGIES, TIPS & TECHNIQUES TO APPLY

Formulating a Hypothesis

Critical thinking is involved in not only formulating a hypothesis, but also in determining whether or not it can be proved or disproved. Formulating a hypothesis comes from careful observation and specific ideas or concepts; reasoning and suppositions can be tested as a result of it. The purpose of this hypothesis formulation is to prove or disprove something through further investigative efforts.

Applying critical thinking for determining a solution to a problem involves hypothesizing to help build a roadmap for approaching the problem realistically and effectively. Breaking down the problem into key drivers or root causes typically helps formulate the hypothesis.

Collecting the Facts

Facts are considered to be meaningful data and information that has merit, or in other words, not false or misleading. Factual information tends to be qualitative or derived from expert opinion or that which is quantitative in nature. From a critical thinking point of view it implies it must be measurable in terms of performance or results. Gathering relevant data and information is a crucial step in supporting the analyses required for proving or disproving the hypothesis.

Within a critical thinking framework, gathering factual, usable information requires knowing: where to dig, how to filter through bits and pieces of collected information, how to verify the data and information through past experiences and utilizations, and how to apply the data and information as it relates to what is attempting to be solved.

Conducting an Analysis

In regard to critical thinking, an analysis is the deliberate process of breaking a problem down through the application of factual knowledge and various diagnostic and investigative techniques. Incorporating an analysis of the facts is required to prove or disprove a hypothesis and provides an understanding of the major issues and drivers behind the problem. It is generally better to spend more time analyzing data and information rather than collecting them. The goal is to find the "gems" that quickly confirm or deny a hypothesis. Completing a root cause analysis, a storyboarding technique, and/or a force field analysis are some of many critical thinking techniques that can be applied effectively.

Developing the Solution

Within the critical thinking framework a solution is defined as the final recommendation presented, which is based on the outcomes of the hypothesis testing process. Solutions are what make or break organizational initiatives, transitions and change. It is important to ensure the solution fits the problem or issues to be decided upon. However, solutions are useless if they cannot be implemented. Running an actual example through the solution is an effective way of testing the effectiveness and viability of it.

How Critical Thinking Is Used
in the Problem Identification Process

A problem becomes known when a person observes a discrepancy between the way things are and the way things ought to be. Problems can be generally identified through: comparative and/or benchmarking examinations, performance reporting, which consists of an assessment of current performance against goals and objectives, a SWOT Analysis, which is an assessment of strengths, weaknesses, opportunities, and threats, analyzing complaints and the factors behind them, and analyzing surveys.

Getting to the "Root" of the Problem

From a critical thinking frame of reference, root causes are defined as a specific underlying cause, which can reasonably be identified and that decision making can control or remedy. It is always important to remember that sometimes what is thought of as the problem requiring a decision is not the real problem at all. It will take critical thinking and reasoning to get at the real causes behind a particular problem and considerable probing may be necessary to identify a root cause.

Applying various techniques like the ones below are also extremely helpful to identify root causes:

The Five Why Technique
The Five Why Technique refers to the practice of asking, five times, why the problem exists. This is useful for quickly getting to the root cause of the problem.

A Root Cause Analysis
This is an effective method of probing, since it helps to identify what, how, and why something occurred, such as creating a cause and effect chart or diagram. A cause and effect diagram is an analysis tool that provides a systematic way of looking at effects and the causes that create or factor into to those effects. The value of the cause and effect diagram is that it provides a method for categorizing the many potential causes of prob-

lems or issues in an orderly way. Through analytical thinking and reasoning the process leads to effectively identifying actual root causes.

A Force Field Analysis
A Force Field Analysis visually illustrates the forces that work to impact a problem or issue.

Process Mapping
Process Mapping tends to chart the "as is" flow of activities that make up a process. It is effective for identifying excessive handoffs, redundancies, and other root causes of inefficiencies.

Benchmarking
Benchmarking works effectively to compare existing performance to another internal or external source, which identifies issues not otherwise revealed through other types of techniques.

Be on the Watch for Some Critical Thinking Pitfalls

Once a problem is defined, decision makers must have some ability to develop a possible solution. If decision makers have little or no control to make recommendations for a problem, then the problem has been defined outside the scope of the project. The initial definition of the problem may not be correct or some involved individuals may lack critical thinking knowledge and experience that more experienced decision makers have. However, since some problems can be totally unique, more experienced decision makers may need to be called upon to validate the problem and possible solutions against other sources (past projects, other experts, etc).

The best solutions to a problem are sometimes too difficult or complex to fully implement. Because of this it is important to be careful about recommending the optimal solution to a problem. Keep in mind that most decision making efforts as well as solutions will require some degree of compromise for implementation.

POINTS TO PONDER — SOMETHING TO THINK ABOUT

1. Have you ever rushed out to collect information before you knew what facts and data to collect in terms of the decision making and/or problem solving technique(s) you planned to use? If so, what was the result of doing this?

2. Do you make it a point to test your solutions through the active use of critical thinking as much as you can? Why or why not?

TRAINING ACTIVITY — APPLICATION & ACTION PLAN

Applying tools and techniques for conducting an analysis is a major element of the critical thinking part of the decision making process. It helps to "make sense" of the factual information collected.

Define a problem or issue that requires a solution or decision developed.

Conduct a critical thinking analysis by determining:

- What things help to clearly define the issues surrounding the problem and solution-driven decision?
- What are the most important issues to address?
- What forces are able to influence the problem?
- What are the core factors and influences related to the problem?
- What areas are weak?

Once this is completed, match up the clearly defined questions and/or issues with the appropriate analytical tool to determine root causes and possible solutions.

6

Understanding and Applying the Components of Critical Thinking

ritical Thinking is a powerful process if understood and applied effectively. When developing critical thinking skills, it is important to understand more about the activity and process that comprises it. Once understood, fears about actively applying critical thinking skills will likely dissipate. Critical thinking is able to translate the thinking process into clear, persuasive, truthful language, which is carefully and logically crafted. At the same time it is able to convert perceptions and reactions into concepts, ideas, assumptions, suppositions, inferences, hypotheses, questions, beliefs, premises and logical arguments.

IMPLICATIONS — WHAT THIS MEANS TO YOU

There are many misconceptions about critical thinking that tend to hinder individuals from continually working to develop it. Unfortunately many assume the process is too difficult and remain unenlightened as to how the process can help them not only in their work environments, but in their own personal lives as well.

Four roadblocks often create negative feelings about getting more involved in the critical thinking process:

- It is more of a negative process, since it tends to tear down ideas and inserts nothing in their place. In actuality, it is a positive process that is able to put things in a more realistic perspective.

- It will lead to the inability to make commitments to people or ideas. In actuality, commitments become informed ones.
- It seems to involve traumatic change since one is expected to continually abandon old assumptions. In actuality, some beliefs stay the same individuals simply become more informed.
- It is detached, unemotional and cold. In actuality, it is highly poignant and liberating, since individuals tend to be free of their past assumptions and the anxiety of self-scrutiny.

▨ STRATEGIES, TIPS & TECHNIQUES TO APPLY

Critical Thinking Encompasses Specific Elements

Every process or method is made of essential components, and critical thinking is no different. These components provide a structure to the process, which if incorporated, makes persuasive, truthful and supportive verbal communication possible to highly influence others' points of view and message acceptance. The major components in critical thinking include: perception, assumptions, emotion, language, argument, fallacy, logic, and problem solving.

Perception

Perception is considered to be the manner in which individuals receive, interpret and translate experiences. How individuals perceive things works to define how they think. Perception tends to provide individuals a significant filtering system.

Assumptions

Assumptions are central to critical thinking. They tend to be implied, where individuals are not always conscious of them. Assumptions are not always bad and often rest on the notion that some ideas are obvious. They tend to make individuals comfortable with their present beliefs, shutting out any alternatives.

Emotion

Trying to leave emotion out of almost anything is impossible as it is part of everything people do and think. Emotions are the number one cause of creating and putting into place thinking and operating barriers, which are continually used as a defense mechanism. Critical thinkers do not ignore or deny emotions but learn to accept and manage them.

Language

Thinking can't be separated from language since both tend to have three primary purposes: to inform, persuade and explain. Language denotes (designates meanings) and connotes (implies or suggests something), and relies heavily on the use of metaphors. Metaphors are powerful language tools, which are able to influence how individuals think and problem solve. These figures of speech give great color and depth to one's language. Metaphors can be short phrases, stories, or even poetic renditions and is a verbal message that listeners can easily interpret and visualize.

Argument

An argument is a claim, which is used to persuade that something is (or is not) true, or should (or should not) be done. An argument contains three basic elements: an issue, one or more reasons or premises, and one or more conclusions. An argument can be either valid or invalid based on its structure and only premises & conclusions are reached, which are either true or false.

The goal of critical thinking is to implement a sound argument, which has both a valid or proper structure and contains true premises. This is where using logic makes all the difference.

Fallacy

Reasoning that doesn't meet the criteria for being a sound argument is considered erroneous, or fallacious. A fallacy comes from incorrect patterns of reasoning. However, it does not always mean that the conclusion is false, but it does underscore the fact that the reasoning used to support it is not: valid, based on true premises, or complete and does not include all necessary relevant information.

Logic

Logic incorporates two methods or types of reasoning: deductive and inductive. Deductive reasoning relies on facts, certainty, syllogisms, validity, truth of premises sound arguments and supported conclusions. Inductive reasoning relies on diverse facts, probability, generalizations, hypotheses, analogies and inductive strength.

Problem Solving Through Logic

A logic problem is like any problem. It requires:
- Understanding the problem. In other words, listen, read & take heed.
- Identifying all of the "unknowns" as well as the "knowns."
- Interpreting relationships between them (visual aids can help).
- Generating a strategy from steps two and three.
- Applying the strategy and solving the problem.
- Repeating the process if it is necessary.

Applying Approaches to Good Critical Thinking

To become a critical and creative thinker there are certain requirements individuals need to take seriously and to practice on a consistent basis. These include:
- Having a sense of inquisitiveness about a wide range of issues.
- Having a desire to become and stay well-informed.
- Keeping alert to various opportunities that require or necessitate the use of critical thinking.
- Having self-confidence in one's abilities to reason.
- Having open-mindedness about divergent work related views.
- Having flexibility in considering alternatives & opinions.
- Understanding the opinions of others whether one agrees with them or not.
- Having fair-mindedness in appraising one's and another's reasoning.
- Maintaining honesty in facing one's own biases and prejudices as well as stereotyping or egocentric tendencies.
- Maintaining caution and discretion in suspending, making and altering judgments.

- Having a willingness to reconsider and adjust, modify or alter one's views.
- Demonstrating clarity in stating questions or concerns.
- Maintaining orderliness when working with complexity.
- Having diligence in seeking out relevant information.
- Incorporating reasonableness in selecting and applying criteria.
- Maintaining focused attention on the issue, problem or concern at hand.
- Maintaining personal persistence when going through thinking or reasoning difficulties.
- Maintaining and sustaining precision to the degree it is permitted by the issues, topics or circumstances encountered.

POINTS TO PONDER — SOMETHING TO THINK ABOUT

1. Do you feel you tend to harbor any misconceptions about critical thinking that often hinders you from continually working to develop it? If so, what are they?
2. Do you believe that thinking can't be separated from language? In what ways are they continually intertwined?

TRAINING ACTIVITY — APPLICATION & ACTION PLAN

Take one situation, problem or issue you wish to work through in a logical, creative manner.

Apply the major components of critical thinking and define, detail and analyze the issue, problem or situation from your own and others':

- Perceptions
- Assumptions
- Emotions
- Language
- Argument
- Fallacy
- Logic
- Problem solving

7

Affective Traits of Critical Thinking

Critical thinking requires more than simply applying one's thinking abilities. Higher order thinking also includes certain attitudes, dispositions and passions, as well as "traits of the mind." These are known as affective traits, which are not merely considered to be important to critical thinking. They are essential for generating abstract thinking and reasoning within real working situations and settings.

The affective traits of critical thinking include:
- Thinking for one's self in an independent manner.
- Exercising impartiality and fair-mindedness as to what is heard, expressed or read.
- Developing personal insights into self-interest and/or self-absorption.
- Developing an intellectual unassuming nature and the ability to suspend judgment.
- Developing intellectual daring and boldness.
- Developing intellectual integrity and trust.
- Developing intellectual resolve and perseverance.
- Developing confidence in one's ability to reason.
- Exploring thoughts that tend to support feelings, as well as feelings that tend to support thoughts.
- Developing intellectual curiosity.

▓ IMPLICATIONS — WHAT THIS MEANS TO YOU

Understanding the affective traits of critical thinking is an important part of incorporating higher order reasoning and thinking. Without independent thought and intellectual perseverance, one could not solve the complicated, multi-faceted problems which confront an organization. Intellectual daring and boldness, as well as the ability to suspend judgment, defend ethics and sound reasoning in the face of threats or chaos. Without a sense of fair-mindedness, intellectual integrity and trust as well as exploring thoughts that tend to support feelings, one would find it nearly impossible to enter into another's point of view to see things as the other person sees and understands things. Fair-mindedness, intellectual integrity and trust work together to create empathetic understanding that is necessary to bring about a reasonable approach to solving problems, conflict as well as other important issues. Without developing insights in regard to elements of self-interest, it becomes extremely easy to succumb to employing reasoning in a highly self-serving, manipulative and prejudiced way. Finally, If you don't possess a sense of confidence in your ability to reason, it becomes extremely difficult, if not impossible, to adequately address highly complex and frequently ambiguous problems that require reasonable decisions in the face of chaos or uncertainty.

▓ STRATEGIES, TIPS & TECHNIQUES TO APPLY

Self-Assessing One's Traits and Abilities of Critical Thinking

Elements of thought do not exist in isolation from one another. Within superior critical thinking, skills that are more closely associated with "elements of thought" become orchestrated into a larger sphere of skills and abilities. These elements of thought can be directly applied to thinking in relationship to more complex and oftentimes ambiguous issues, problems, decisions, theories, particular states of circumstances, organizational implications, and/or human actions. It is important to analyze whether the various elements of thought are actively practiced on a continuous basis.

Effective critical thinking includes becoming skillful in its application through:

- Refining generalizations and avoiding over-simplifications
- Comparing similar types of situations in order to transfer insights into new contexts
- Developing one's own personal perspective through creating or exploring the implications of beliefs, arguments, methods or theories
- Clarifying issues, conclusions or beliefs
- Clarifying and analyzing the meanings of words and phrases
- Developing criteria for evaluation, which includes clarifying values and standards
- Evaluating the credibility of sources of information
- Questioning deeply by raising and pursuing root or significant questions
- Analyzing or evaluating arguments, interpretations, beliefs, methods, concepts or theories
- Generating or assessing solutions
- Analyzing or evaluating actions, procedures, methods, issues or policies
- Reasoning dialogically or thoroughly by comparing perspectives, interpretations, methods, concepts or theories
- Reasoning dialectically or diagnostically by evaluating perspectives, interpretations, methods, concepts or theories
- Reading critically by constructing an accurate interpretation, as well as understanding the elements of thought in what is written, which also includes evaluating the reasoning behind it
- Listening critically to construct an accurate interpretation of what is being stated as well as understanding the elements of thought in what is being presented. It also includes internally evaluating the reasoning behind the oral communication
- Writing critically by creating, developing, clarifying, and conveying in written form, the logic of one's thinking
- Speaking critically by creating, developing, clarifying, and effectively conveying the logic behind one's thinking

Developing Proficiency in One's Critical Thinking Abilities

- Combining and effectively applying various critical thinking abilities is critical for generating:
- The capacity to make sound decisions, to participate knowledgeably in the workplace, and to effectively function as part of a collective group of individuals.
- The capacity to master solving complex issues and problems as well as to make insightful connections, and to communicate effectively.

Both of the above relies heavily on having and utilizing a significant number of these listed abilities. For example, the capacity to make sound decisions: such decision making is hardly possible without the ability to (going down the list of abilities in order) refine generalizations, compare analogous situations, thoroughly develop one's perspective, and to clarify issues.

Reading, writing, listening, and speaking, when applied in a critical, informed and constructive way, need to be considered as actual "styles and approaches" to constructive, abstract thinking. As such, they need to be looked upon as structured mixes of basic skills that become interwoven with numerous other critical thinking abilities.

Critical thinking requires individuals to be able to perform with a level of expertise that is appropriate for approaching various organizational issues and situations. Proficiency in critical thinking includes having the ability to:

- Identify a plausible statement of a speaker's or writer's purpose
- Rank formulations of a speaker's or author's objectives
- Distinguish clearly between purposes, consequences, assumptions, and inferences
- Choose the most reasonable statement of the problem that a speaker or an author is presenting or addressing
- Reasonably discuss the qualities, worth and merits of different versions or sides of the question at issue
- Recognize common key elements in formulations of different problems
- Give a clear articulation of a speaker's or writer's point of view
- Identify the most reasonable statement of a speaker's or writer's point of view

- Recognize bias, narrowness, and contradictions in the point of view being expressed or presented
- Identify assumptions and implications of a speaker's or writer's point of view
- Distinguish evidence from conclusions which are based on that evidence
- Give evidence to back up a speaker's or writer's position
- Recognize information that would support, information that would oppose as well as information that would be considered neutral with respect to a given position
- Recognize conclusions that go beyond the evidence
- Note, in an evaluative manner, the presence or absence of evidence
- Identify the main concepts within a presentation or supportive statement or rebuttal
- Distinguish main concepts from nonessential or secondary ones
- Identify the assumption underlying a given inference
- Evaluate the suitability or appropriateness of different versions of an assumption
- Distinguish between inferences and assumptions
- Rank different formulations of assumptions with respect to which is the most reasonable
- Identify crucial implications of a statement or passage
- Discriminate between consequences that are necessary, probable, and improbable
- Evaluate personal inferences
- Make justified inferences
- Choose the most accurate version of a speaker's or writer's inferences
- Draw reasonable inferences from positions the speaker or writer disagrees with

Applying One's Critical Thinking Abilities

Abilities that are grounded in a thorough familiarity with the elements of thought, tend to become the activities one actually applies to perform higher order thinking. Abilities like clarifying values and standards, comparing analogous situations, generating and assessing solutions, analyzing and evaluating actions, methods, concepts, procedures and policies are the outcomes of reasoning. These abilities are the means by which decisions are made, problems are solved, thinking in the workplace is strengthened, and from which greater understandings of rights, accountability, and responsibility become deepened.

The abilities of critical reading, writing and speaking can be viewed as the cornerstones of assessing and evaluating higher order thinking. To read, write and speak critically requires being able to clarify values, compare analogous situations, and to exercise other critical thinking abilities, mixed with various elements of thought. These work together in order to generate ideas, solutions and much more.

Why Self-Assessment Is Important

Self-assessment for measuring one's proficiency in critical thinking can be keyed to individual performance as well as personal and intellectual growth. Without self-assessing one's abilities and traits, only a diminished idea or concept of critical thinking tends to become addressed rather than its whole process. What allows individuals to solve their problems in an effective, conscientious and industrious way as well as address complicated, intricate real-life or work problems diligently, objectively, and logically, is not just done by simply applying one's thinking and reasoning abilities. It is accomplished by applying one's intellectual perseverance, drive or disposition, which is an affective trait. A similar point can be made for one's intellectual traits, which are the driving force behind sound, insightful and acute reasoning.

Doing a self-assessment of one's critical thinking traits needs to concentrate on identifying, measuring and altering if necessary, one's aspects of fair-mindedness, a willingness to suspend judgment, intellectual daring and boldness, as well as intellectual integrity and trust. Proficiency in critical thinking in regard to the intellectual standards attached to it requires individuals to:

- Recognize clarity from blurred reasoning, inferences and implications and supportive statements
- Distinguish accurate from inaccurate explanations and/or descriptions and documentation
- Decide when a statement is relevant or irrelevant in regard to a given point
- Identify inconsistent positions as well as relatively consistent ones

- Discriminate deep, thorough, and significant explanations, descriptions and accounts from those that are superficial, fragmentary, and trivial
- Assess and evaluate responses with respect to their fairness
- Prefer well-evidenced accounts to those that are unsupported by factual evidence
- Discern good reasons from bad

POINTS TO PONDER — SOMETHING TO THINK ABOUT

1. Higher order thinking includes certain attitudes, dispositions and passions, as well as traits of the mind. From your personal viewpoint, what does this phrase mean and imply?
2. In what ways do you feel the affective traits of critical thinking impacts higher order reasoning and thinking? Why?

TRAINING ACTIVITY — APPLICATION & ACTION PLAN

Take one issue or problem to address using the following elements of thought and your abilities of critical thinking.

Use them to define:

1. The intended purpose or goal in regard to the problem being solved
   Remember: If a goal is unrealistic, contradictory, confusing, or mixed-up in some way to other goals one has, then the reasoning used to achieve that goal is problematic.

2. The question "at issue" that needs to be decided upon and solved
   Remember: Whenever there is an attempt to reason something out, there is at least one question at issue, and at least one problem that needs to be resolved. One area of concern will be the formulation of

this particular question, whether it is in regard to one's own reasoning or that of others.

3. Points of view or frames of reference
    Remember: Whenever an individual reasons, he or she must reason within some point of view, or frame of reference. Any "defect" in this point of view or frame of reference will create possible problems in the reasoning and decision making process. A point of view may be too narrow, too unsophisticated or closed-minded, or it may be based on false or misleading information, misrepresented analogies, inappropriate metaphors, or possible contradictions etc.

4. Assumptions
    Remember: All reasoning must begin somewhere, and must take some things for granted. Any "defect" in comprehending underlying assumptions or presuppositions with which the reasoning is built, can generate multiple problems.

5. Implications and consequences
    Remember: No matter where one stops his or her reasoning, it will always have further implications and consequences. As reasoning develops, statements will logically be entailed by it. Any "defect" in the implications or consequences of one's reasoning is a possible source of problems.

6. Inferences
    Remember: Reasoning proceeds in steps, by which an individual reasons as follows: "Because this is so ... that also is so (or is probably so)," or "Since this ... therefore that." Any "defect" in such inferences is able to generate a possible problem within the reasoning process.

8

Critical Thinking – the Process of Framing and Reframing

ritical thinking and working effectively with others relies on applying appropriate frames. Frames are cognitive short-cuts that individuals use to help make sense out of complex information and to interpret that information in a way that can be meaningfully represented to others. Frames help to organize complex experiences, occurrences and facts into logical and rational as well as understandable groupings and categories. By labeling these complex experiences, occurrences and facts it becomes possible to give meaning to some aspects of what is observed through them, while at the same time discounting other aspects because they appear to be irrelevant or counterintuitive. Frames provide meaning through selective simplification, by filtering people's perceptions and providing them with a field of vision for a problem.

▦ IMPLICATIONS – WHAT THIS MEANS TO YOU

Frames significantly impact the critical thinking process. This is because they tend to be built upon personal beliefs, values, and experiences, where individuals often construct unique frames that tend to considerably vary. Frames normally exist prior to the processing of information and they highly affect identifying, assessing, analyzing, and evaluating information, upon which critical thinking is based.

Individuals tend to be separated not only by differences in personal interests, beliefs, and values, but also in how they perceive and understand things, both at a conscious as well as sub-conscious level. Within critical thinking, individuals generally apply framing not only as an aid to interpreting issues and information, but also at times, to generate or promote some form of a strategic advantage.

Framing is often the impetus for rationalizing self-interest, convincing others, building unity, or promoting a preference for a specific outcome. Numerous factors tend to affect how people frame experiences, situations and circumstances, which in turn, influences the path and direction that critical thinking takes.

▦ STRATEGIES, TIPS & TECHNIQUES TO APPLY

The Importance of Framing When Thinking Critically

An essential element in critical thinking is understanding how and why frames affect decision making or problem solving development. In the context of critical thinking situations, disagreements often erupt. As a result, individuals tend to create frames to help understand why the disagreement exists, what actions are important to alter or negate it, why different individuals act as they do, and how individuals should act in response to what is occurring.

Within group situations and activities, frames serve as a type of strainer for information that is being gathered, assembled and analyzed. Personal framing tends to determine the development of priorities and ways to address and achieve them, which typically includes generating alternative solutions as well particular action plans for their implementation. Depending on the issue, problem or context of the task or goal at hand, framing may be used to conceptualize and interpret, or to manipulate and convince.

Framing tends to be tied to information processing, message patterns, linguistic cues, and socially constructed meanings. Knowing what the various types of frames are, and how they are constructed, allows individuals to draw conclusions about how they affect the development of critical thinking and its outcomes, as well as how they can be used to influence both. It is important to analyze existing frames from a personal perspective, as well as ones others use. Doing this offers fresh insight into the dynamics and development of group interaction, problem solving, conflict resolution as well as decision making.

The Sources and Forms of Frames

Many factors work to influence frames as well as their formation. Disagreements and opposite viewpoints are usually associated with a complex and reinforcing set of frames in oneself, and others, as well as associated elements of risk, what types of information should be applied to a given situation, and how decisions should be made. The frames that most highly influence disagreements and opposing viewpoints among individuals include ones of: identity, characterization, power, risk/information, and loss versus gain.

Identity Frames

Individuals tend to view themselves as having particular identities in the context of specific circumstances and situations. These identities spring from an individual's self-conception and group affiliation. The more central the challenge to one's sense of self, the more oppositional one is likely to act. Typical responses to threats to identity include ignoring information and perspectives that tend to threaten one's core identity, reinforcing connections with like-minded individuals or groups, and negatively characterizing problems, issues or situations.

Characterization Frames

Closely related to stereotyping, characterization frames may be either positive or negative. Individuals view others as having particular characteristics and when they find themselves in disagreement or at odds with others often tend to construct characterization frames for them that significantly differ from how the other parties view themselves. Such characterizations often undermine others' legitimacy, and cast doubt on their motivations, or exploit their sensitivity.

Characterization frames often tend to be linked to identity frames, which serve to strengthen one's personal identity while justifying individual actions toward another, thinking for example, "I am a free thinker, but my opponent is closed-minded and because of it needs to be subdued or chastised."

Power Frames

Because disagreement is often imbedded into critical thinking activities like decision making, individual conceptions of power and group control tend to play a significant role in them. Power frames help a disagreer determine which forms of power are justifiable, such as in the form of existing organizational structure. At the same time, power frames also help to determine certain forms of power that are likely to advance one's own agenda or positioning, like authority, resources, expertise, or unity-building.

Risk and Information Frames

Disagreements that often erupt during critical thinking projects or activities often involve personal expectations about future events, where these events may either be risky, or where the likelihood of them occurring is quite uncertain. Within these types of situations, certain group members will often begin to construct risk and information frames that produce highly variable assessments about the level and extent of a particular risk.

From a positive viewpoint, risk and information frames work to indicate which sources of information tend to be reliable, and which ones are not. Risk and information frames depend not just on an individual's points of interest, but also on the person's level of training, expertise, personal exposure to the risk, familiarity with the risk, and the potential for disastrous or negative impacts due to it. Because of the ability to deeply analyze various risk factors and their potential consequences these critical thinkers tend to act and think in terms of the degree in which the risk is dreaded or feared.

Loss Versus Gain Frames

It is common for most individuals who work as a collective group in problem solving or decision making to focus on "threats of potential loss," rather than on "opportunities for gain." People tend to react differently to a proposed course of action when its expected consequences are framed in terms of "losses" as opposed to "gains." Most times there will be individuals who hold firm to believing that preventing a perceived loss is much more relevant, significant, and high in value than securing an equal gain. This works to reinforce a psychological barrier in regard to taking a particular course of action or accepting a specific problem's solution.

Reframing

Reframing is the process of purposefully managing one's personal frames. With the help of reframing, individuals are more likely to find new ways to reach an agreement. Within critical thinking activities such as decision making or problem solving, the ability to effectively manage frames and the framing process can lead to important shifts not only in the frames themselves, but also in the impact that they have on group dynamics.

Reframing is intended to:
- Clarify various viewpoints in order to bring about a more productive exchange of information by listening to ideas that were not previously considered. This includes expanding discussions to explore different courses of action or solutions that had not been previously addressed.
- Enhance individuals' understanding of their interests and how the forms of action they take are used to serve these interests, which is accomplished by examining potential processes for managing frames more productively and to reconsider patterns of interaction among other group members.
- Identify concepts, issues, or informational areas that individuals tend to view differently, which is used to determine opportunities for compromise, negotiation or trade-offs, which can be based on these specific differences.
- Identify differences to determine which ones cannot be bridged. As an essential part of reframing it becomes important to identify ways to reduce or eliminate areas of disagreement in a manner that does not violate these types of differences, which includes determining the degree of importance that is awarded to them.

TRAINING ACTIVITY — APPLICATION & ACTION PLAN

1. A Frame Analysis can be used to better manage disagreement and to advance consensus building through the analysis of issues and their associated consequences.
2. Take the time to do a Frame Analysis at your next group meeting when a disagreement erupts.
3. Begin by:
    - Establishing a common ground as a basis for agreement through focusing on a smaller set of issues in relationship to the big picture.
    - Exploring areas of agreement and possible joint action between parties who normally focus on their differences, in order to open up communication between the parties.
    - Identifying desired future possibilities, outcomes and opportunities in order to shift the focus from a short-term perspective to a long-term one.
    - Enhancing the desirability of options and alternatives through the application of divergent frames. Allow yourself to examine options from other framing perspectives. Make it a point to understand others' frames, and view possible options from their perspectives.
    - Exploring with others the meaning and impact of personal frames on the group dynamics process. This includes focusing on the factors and issues that can lead to changes within

a frame, or changes to the frames themselves. In this sense, framing tends to become a formative analytic technique.

- Exploring ways that can lead to reframing perceptions in terms of "losses versus gains," which is necessary to enhance the openness and creativity of the group critical thinking project or activity.

Keep in mind that frames are often quite stable over time, even when individuals find themselves moving in and out of different types of situations. This is because they are continuously self-reinforced and because these frames are often shared by others, which are then supported through shared perspectives. Yet is always important to remember that frames can be altered over time.

Reframing is not always an easy process. It requires taking on new perspectives, which involves some degree of risk taking. Reframing works best when changes in the context of an issue or problem can be made, which makes it possible to consider new perspectives, or by altering a situation to reflect constructive dialogue, where it contains a strong focus on improving communication and building trust.

About the Author

Timothy F. Bednarz, Ph.D. is CEO of the American Management Development Group, Inc. For over 20 years he has researched, designed and authored hundreds of learning and development programs used by Fortune 1000 companies.

He is also the author of *Great! What Makes Leaders Great. What They Did, How They Did It and What You Can Learn from It* (2011).

Speaking Availability

Timothy F. Bednarz, Ph.D. is available for speaking engagements for your next meeting or association event. He can be contacted at 800-654-4935 or by e-mail at timothy.bednarz@majorium.com.

Bulk Sales

Bulk sales of this book or any other titles available from Majorium Business Press. Inquiries can be directed to sales@majorium.com, or by phone at 800-6654-4935.

Quick Order Form

Fax orders: 715-342-1118. Send this form.

Telephone orders: Call 800-654-4935 toll-free. Have your credit card ready.

Email orders: sales@majorium.com

Postal orders: Majorium Business Press, 2025 Main Street, Stevens Point, WI 54481, USA.

Please send the following books:

_____

_____

_____

_____

Please send more FREE information on:

❑Catalog   ❑Speaking/Seminars   ❑Mailing Lists   ❑Consulting

Name: _____

Address: _____

City: _____ State: _____ Zip: _____

Telephone: _____

Email address: _____

Sales tax: Please add 5.5% for products shipped to Wisconsin addresses.

Shipping by air:

United States: $4.00 for first book and $2.00 for each additional product.

International: $9.00 for first book; $5.00 for each additional product (estimate).

28914652R00037

Printed in Great Britain
by Amazon